What Do You Think?

Contents

What Is It?

Written by Lisa Burton
Illustrated by Mark Wilson

They say it lives in North America.
They say it lives in the woods.
What is it?

They say it looks like a big tall ape person.
It has brown or black hair all over it.
It has long, long arms.
They say it has two big, big feet.
Its feet are bigger than a person's feet.
Its feet are bigger than a gorilla's feet.
Its feet are bigger than a brown bear's feet.
What is it?

They say it eats leaves.
They say it eats little animals.
They say that it goes to sleep in the winter
like the brown bears do.
They say it is very strong.
It can lift things that people can't lift.
They say it makes a sound like a whistle.
They say it is scary.
What is it?

A long time ago, some men were staying in the woods.
One man saw a big tall animal.
The animal looked like a person.
The animal had brown hair all over it.
The animal ran at the man.
The man got his gun and shot the animal.
The man went to his cabin to tell the other men.
The men went outside to look.
There were more of the big tall animals
coming up to the cabin.
The men ran inside the cabin.
They shut all the cabin doors
and all the shutters on the cabin windows.
The animals banged on the doors
and banged on the shutters.
Then the animals went up onto the roof.
They banged on the roof.
Then the animals got some rocks
and banged them on the walls.
They banged on the walls all night.
When it was daytime,
the animals stopped banging and went away.
What are they?

A long time ago, a man went into the woods
to look for gold.
When he was asleep, something picked him up
and took him away.
When the sun came up,
the man saw four big tall animals looking at him.
They all had long arms and big hands and big feet.
They had brown hair all over them.
The man said they looked like people.
He said it was a father and a mother and two children.
He stayed for two weeks.
Then he got away.

How do you
think the man
got away?

Are they animals?
Are they monsters?
Are they giants?
Are they real?
Do they come from space?
There are lots of stories about this animal.
Because lots of people say
that they have seen its big footprints,
they call it *Bigfoot*.
Because a lot of people say
that it is wild, they call it *Sasquatch*.
Sasquatch means *wild man of the woods*.

What do you think?

Where Did They Go?

Written by David Chang
Illustrated by Bryan Pollard

The Bermuda Triangle is a strange place.
The Bermuda Triangle is part of the sea
between Bermuda, Puerto Rico, and Florida.

Lots of ships have sunk in the Bermuda Triangle.
Lots of planes have crashed in the Bermuda Triangle.
The ships and the planes
were missing without a trace.

Look on the atlas.
See if you can find
the Bermuda
Triangle.

Bermuda •

• Florida

Puerto Rico •

11

1918

One ship was missing. The weather was good.
No trace of the ship was found.
No bodies were found.

1925

Two ships were missing.
No trace of them was found.
No bodies were found.

1944

Seven planes were flying
in the Bermuda Triangle.
They were thrown around in the air.
Two of the planes got back to land.
Five of the planes were
missing without a trace.

1945

Seven planes were missing.
No trace of them was found.
No bodies were found.

1920   **1930**   **1940**

1948

Near Miami, one plane was missing. No trace of it was found. No bodies were found.
Near Bermuda, two planes were missing.
No trace of them was found. No bodies were found.

1953

A big tanker was missing. A plank from the tanker was found on the beach.
No bodies were found.

1968

A submarine was missing.
99 men were on the submarine.
The submarine was found on the ocean floor months later. No cause for the disaster could be found.

1969

A woman was flying her plane.
She said she was lost.
She and her plane were never seen again.

1950   **1960**   **1970**

Why do all these ships and planes
end up missing without a trace?
Why do they go missing in the Bermuda Triangle?

Some people think
that the sea in the Bermuda Triangle is strange.
The sea in the Bermuda Triangle
has hot and cold streams running in it.
When the hot and cold streams hit each other,
it makes the sea rough.

Some people think
that the air in the Bermuda Triangle is strange.
The air makes big storms.
A big storm can make a compass go wrong.
A compass tells the pilots where they are going.
If the pilots do not know where they are going,
they may fly the plane out to sea.
If the pilots fly the plane too far away,
the plane may run out of fuel and crash into the sea.

If a big storm and the streams of hot and cold water
meet, they can make a big waterspout.
A waterspout is like a tornado at sea.
A waterspout could suck a plane or a ship right inside it.

Some people think
that the people who made the ships and the planes
may have made mistakes.
Maybe the ships and the planes broke into pieces.

Some people think
that the people on the planes and the ships
may have made mistakes.
If a pilot makes a bad mistake, the plane could crash.

Some people think
that the planes and ships are taken away
by people in spaceships.

What do you think?

What are four things
that people think make
planes and ships go
missing in the Bermuda
Triangle?

How Did He Get Out?

Written by Howard Gothard
Illustrated by Mary Ann Hurley

One day, my dad said we could go to see Harry Houdini.
We went into town.
We went to the place where Harry Houdini was going to be.
Lots of people were there.
Lots of people had come to see Harry Houdini escape.
We had good seats.
We could see all the things Harry Houdini was doing.

Harry Houdini came onto the stage.
He had a woman with him.
She was Harry Houdini's helper.
We all clapped our hands.
The woman put some handcuffs
on Harry Houdini's wrists.
She locked the handcuffs with a key.
She threw the key away.
Then Harry Houdini was out of the handcuffs.
How did he do it?
We clapped and clapped our hands.

Harry Houdini put the handcuffs
on the woman's wrists.
The woman got into a big wooden box.
Harry Houdini shut the lid of the box.
He tied the box up with rope.

How do you think Harry Houdini got the handcuffs off?

Harry Houdini went behind the curtain.
Then, bang!
The woman came out from behind the curtain.
She pulled the curtain open.

The woman untied the rope
and opened the box.
Harry Houdini got out of the box.
How did he do it?
We clapped and clapped our hands.

Harry Houdini's helper got a big can.
The can was bigger than Harry Houdini.
She filled up the can with water.
Harry Houdini said he was going to get in the can.
The woman put the handcuffs
on Harry Houdini's wrists.
Then Harry Houdini
got into the can.
He went under the water.

The woman put the top on the can and locked it.
She pulled the small curtain in front of the can.
We waited and waited. Where was Harry Houdini?
What was Harry Houdini doing?
We waited and waited.

There was a loud bang, and there was Harry Houdini.
He was all wet.
We clapped and clapped our hands.

I asked my dad how Harry Houdini got out of the can.
My dad said he did not know.
I asked my mother and my sisters and my brothers.
They did not know how Harry Houdini got out.

Do you know?

Who Built It?

Written by Kerrie Capobianco
Illustrated by Bryan Pollard

Stonehenge is in England.
Stonehenge is a ring of big stones.
The ring has 300 big stones.
The stones are two times taller than a person.
The stones are as heavy as nine elephants.
People think that Stonehenge
was made more than 3,500 years ago.

No one knows who built Stonehenge.
No one knows how Stonehenge was made.
No one knows why Stonehenge was made.

People have been trying to find out
about Stonehenge for a long, long time.
This is what some people think.

They think that it took more than 1,500 years
to build Stonehenge.
They think that it must have taken
thousands and thousands of people.

How do you think the stones got to Stonehenge?

First the people would have had to find the stones. The stones that make up Stonehenge came from as far as 30 miles (48 km) away. The people would have had to find a way to carry the stones that far.

There were no trucks to put the stones in.
The people who built Stonehenge
must have had to push or pull the stones.
They may have made some rope from vines
to help them pull the stones.

How did the people dig the big holes
to stand the stones in?
They did not have shovels to dig the holes.
They had little stones and sticks.

How do you think they dug the holes and cut the stones?

The stones in the ring are all the same shape.
The people had to cut the stones.
How did they cut the stones?
They did not have power tools.
They had tools made of stone or wood.

Why did they build Stonehenge?
Some people think
that it was like
a kind of church
for the people to go to.

Some people think it was to tell the time.
The people who built Stonehenge
looked between the stones.
They saw where the sun was.
They told the time by where the sun was.

What do you think?

Index